To Nita,
Happy Holiday
Happy
Summer Sriduma

*Simona Sez:*

"Home is Where We Go for Refueling."

# *Simona Sez:*

# "Home is Where We Go for Refueling."

SIMONA A. SEIDERMAN, LMSW, DCSW, BCD

BEN REED PUBLISHING
USA

Copyright 2010 Simona A. Seiderman
All rights reserved

Artwork copyright 2011
Ben Reed Publishing Company, LLC

Library of Congress Control Number: 2011902173

ISBN 978-0-9845091-4-0

Published in the United States of America
Ben Reed Publishing Company LLC, 2011

Edited by Rachel E. Seiderman
Designed by Thomas Church

To Abraham, my husband, and
Rachel, Sarah, and Daniel, my children,
whose life stories have been entwined
with mine.


And to all of the people who have entrusted me
with the stories of their lives.

## Contents

Introduction

I. Me, Myself, and I     1

II. Family and Relationships     49

III Grief and Loss     99

Index     133

## INTRODUCTION

In my thirty years of experience as a clinical social worker, I have had the honor and privilege of working with a variety of client populations. Although clients may present with similar issues, each person has a unique personality and history, so each therapeutic experience is different. These variations in therapeutic relationships have given me new insights into life.

Though I am an agent of change, I cannot *make* anyone change. As a therapist, I am a tool for people who wish to engage in the process of change.

*I was destined to be a therapist.*

I was born in 1951, four years after the death of my maternal grandfather. The tradition of the Ashkenazi branch of Judaism is to name after the dead. My parents named me in memory of my grandfather, whose name was Simon Abraham—I was given the name Simona Allison.

Rabbi Shraga Simmons, in an article titled, "A name defines a person's essence. Choose carefully," states that, "The naming of a Jewish child is a most profound spiritual moment. The Sages say that naming a baby is a statement of her character, her specialness, and her path in life."

My path in life was clear: Simona means *one who hears*.

According to Jewish custom, I was also given a Hebrew name. A week after I was born, my family attended Shabbat services at our synagogue. My father was called to the Torah, where a prayer of health was said for me and my mother; then my Hebrew name, Sima Bracha, was publicly proclaimed. Sima means *treasure*. Bracha means *blessing*.

My Hebrew name adds to my identity and connects me to my religion, my grandfather, and all of my ancestors. My English and Hebrew names define me not only as a treasured blessing, but one who hears others – important credentials for a therapist in the making.

Other important credentials include experiencing all that life has to offer: the open roads, the bumps, the obstacles, and the walls that stop you dead in your tracks. Luckily for me, I have experienced them all!

And it's not just experiencing the joy and pain of life that makes you a good therapist; it's what you do with the experiences. Hopefully, you use them to discover more about yourself, and, in the process, learn more effective ways of dealing with life.

I spent many years in therapy learning about myself: my strengths, my weaknesses, and my defenses. Being a patient can be a very painful, exhausting experience, but it can be exhilarating, too. For a future therapist, it's a great opportunity to learn all the nuances of the therapeutic relationship firsthand.

After completing my undergraduate and graduate degrees, I attended postgraduate classes to further my understanding of the therapeutic process. I also spent many years in supervision, a process through which I discovered more about myself as a person and as a therapist.

During my lifetime, I have experienced abandonment, hunger, homelessness, depression, anxiety, insecurity, unbridled fear, profound grief, discrimination, and humiliation. I have also experienced love, trust, friendship, acceptance, security, intense joy, laughter, success, and understanding.

I have traveled along the open roads, over the bumps, and around the obstacles of life. Sometimes I have had to accept that I couldn't go through a wall; I couldn't climb it; I was powerless. In those situations, I sought a scenic turn out lane where I would have the opportunity to contemplate and work through the issues.

These days, I linger at rest stops when necessary, taking the time to analyze the road before me and adjusting accordingly.

As a therapist, I have lived up to my name: I have heard.

◆

As you read this book, you will see that people sometimes enter therapy when there are bumps, obstacles, or walls in their lives. Therapy gives them the opportunity to explore their issues with a trained, non-judgmental listener. With successful therapy, the bumps in the road become smoother, the obstacles more negotiable, and the walls easier to accept.

I hope the insights I have gleaned will help others successfully navigate the roads of their lives.

# I.

# Me, Myself, and I

> "If I am not for myself, who will be for me?"
>
> Rabbi Hillel, c. 110 BCE - 10 CE

> Simona Sez . . .
>
> "You for you, me for me, we are the only ones in the world charged with the responsibility of taking good care of ourselves."

From moment to moment, each of us is the only one who *really knows* what we are thinking, feeling, and experiencing. We may be thinking about the past, contemplating the future, or we may be bored, sad, tired, hungry, and so on.

From the time we are aware of our current state of being, it is just another step to determine what we want to do. We can choose to meet our needs, postpone them, ask someone else to fulfill them for us, or ignore them.

Case study:

As a young boy, Joe loved taking things apart and putting them back together. When he was a bit older, he tinkered with cars both at home and in the automotive repair class offered by his high school. Following graduation, Joe got the necessary training and became an auto mechanic.

After three years on the job, Joe began to feel restless and dissatisfied at work. He dreamed of returning to school to earn a degree but felt that it would be too much for him – making phone calls and going to new places were activities that filled him with anxiety and dread.

Feeling stuck, Joe decided to seek therapy. His intelligence and insightfulness helped him to understand and work through the barriers keeping him from moving forward with his college education. Exploration in therapy revealed that Joe's problems stemmed from a lifetime of being criticized for having needs of any kind – physiological, emotional, or otherwise.

Therapy helped Joe recognize the interplay between his past and present thoughts, feelings, and experiences. Armed with this knowledge, Joe enrolled in college. Four years later, I received a note from Joe accompanied by an announcement of his college graduation with a degree in mechanical engineering.

> Simona Sez . . .
>
> "Practice makes everything easier."

Everyone has heard the expression, "Practice makes perfect." Belief in this philosophy puts an inordinate amount of pressure on someone to do something that is impossible - be perfect.

My philosophy is, "Practice makes everything easier." I encourage my patients to practice whatever it is they want to improve on, whether it is a behavior (like being more assertive or making more eye contact with others), a skill, a sport, or a hobby. Each time a new behavior is practiced, it is easier to engage in the next time.

Case study:

Gloria was a woman who could never say no. People would ask her to do the most outlandish things, like give them large sums of money, buy them expensive jewelry, or take them to lavish dinners. Gloria recognized that when she gave in to other people's demands, she was depriving herself of the things that were important to her. In therapy, she learned how to be assertive* and say no to others when it was appropriate to do so.

*People who practice being assertive are frequently aggressive at the start and become more assertive over time as they learn to modulate their responses.

> Simona Sez ...
>
> "Positive self-talk and physical soothing are important aspects of nurturing ourselves."

Perhaps you recall the story of Jessica McClure, the eighteen-month-old who fell into a Midland, Texas, well on October 14, 1987. During the 58 hours Jessica was trapped in the well, she was often heard singing nursery rhymes. Jessica was most likely emulating her parent's behavior: Many parents sing to their children when they are upset in order to comfort them.

Unfortunately, not all children have a parent who will offer comfort during difficult times, tuck them in at night, or validate their thoughts, feelings, or experiences. As adults, each of us needs to be able to nurture ourselves. We can do this by soothing ourselves physically, by validating ourselves, or by expressing compassion for ourselves.

Case study:

Emma loved to speak in public, yet always became extremely anxious prior to speaking engagements. Before stepping up to the podium, Emma would say to herself, "I know you're scared, it's okay to be scared, you will be all right after you get started, you will settle down like you always do." That compassion and validation was all Emma needed in order to be able to speak in front of others.

Case study:

Hanna was waiting to be called in for a job interview. She could feel the butterflies multiplying in her stomach and her mouth becoming dry. She knew it was normal to feel anxious about things that are important, but she also knew that she would be able to think more clearly if she could settle herself down. She began reassuring herself about her value as a person, her work experiences, and her skills. By the time she was called in for her interview, she felt much calmer. Hanna did so well at her original interview that she was asked to return for the next round of interviews.

> Simona Sez . . .
>
> "Everything is talkable."

We have all received messages from our family, friends, and society about "taboo topics." Such subjects include sex, mental illness, a family member's use of drugs or alcohol, and suicide attempts or completed suicides.

While advertising the most intimate details of our lives is not acceptable, it is very important that we have at least one confidant in our life who we can share everything with: the good, the bad, and the ugly!

Case study:

Ethan's younger brother, Sam, attempted suicide. His parents found Sam unconscious and called 911. As Sam was being rushed to the hospital, Ethan's parents told him that he was to talk with NO ONE about his brother's suicide attempt.

Without the facts, Ethan was left to fill in the blanks for himself. He was afraid his brother would die. He imagined it was his fault that Sam attempted suicide, as the two of them had quarreled the day before. Ethan was alone with his anxiety, guilt, and fear. He had been admonished not to reach out to anyone.

Years later, in the safe environment of therapy, Ethan was encouraged to talk about his brother's suicide attempt. Finally able to voice all the details of the trauma, he could see that he wasn't responsible for his brother's actions and was freed of the guilt that had plagued him since adolescence.

> Simona Sez . . .
>
> "Just BE."

"BEING" is an elusive phenomena for many people. Our hurried lives, with multiple roles and concurrent responsibilities, leave us little time to sit in silence; this sitting in silence, though, is what allows us to figure out where we really are and to get in touch with ourselves. With practice, BEING can extend to non-quiet times, as well.

BEING takes many forms: BEING alone, BEING fully engaged in a conversation, BEING in the moment, and BEING happy are just a few of the many ways TO BE. Sometimes just being is difficult because we have been taught to always BE PRODUCTIVE; to be a Human DOING instead of a Human BEING! Other times, in the void of being productive, we experience the thoughts and feelings we have been working hard to avoid!

Case study:

Stacy, age 25, lived with her parents until she graduated from college and secured a full-time job. She began therapy because she was very anxious about being alone after she moved into her own home. Even the distraction of the television was not enough to quell her anxiety.

Stacy came to understand that she was trying to avoid feeling vulnerable. In addition to instituting appropriate safety measures, Stacy learned how to comfort herself when she was anxious. By the time therapy terminated, Stacy was able to enjoy quiet time in her home.

> Simona Sez . . .
>
> "Who controls your self-esteem?"

Our self-esteem has its building blocks in infancy, based on our caregiver's messages to us through mirroring. We feel lovable when our caregivers consistently look at us lovingly. On the contrary, if our caregivers are depressed or pay little attention to us, we feel we are NOT lovable.

These early experiences lay the foundation for our self-esteem. In the first instance, we feel good about ourselves and grow up regulating our own self-esteem. In the latter, we feel "bad" about ourselves and grow older allowing others to have control over how we feel about ourselves.

Case study:

Judy's mother was depressed before and after Judy's birth. She spent little time with Judy, propping her bottle when it was feeding time and only taking care of her basic needs. While Judy was growing up, her sisters always told her she was bad and stupid. They also took great delight in hiding Judy's favorite blanket from her.

As an adult, if anyone even questioned her, Judy automatically felt unworthy and stupid. Whenever there was static on the radio, she'd feel responsible for it. In other words, she allowed others to control how she felt about herself rather than evaluating and making her own decisions about her worthiness and level of intelligence.

> Simona Sez . . .
>
> "Bad things happen all around us as we sit by innocently and have no control over them – however, <u>we are responsible</u> for creating the good times."

For just a moment, recall the Oklahoma City bombing of 1995, the horror of 9/11, and the devastation of Hurricane Katrina. Each of these events left scores of people dead, injured, or displaced. This is what I mean when I say that bad things happen all around us and we have no control over them. Bad things happen on a smaller scale, too, like the life-threatening diagnosis of a friend or the death of a family member.

Because there are so many things in our lives we have no control over, we need to make time to enjoy life. It is important to take time with family and friends, to engage in pleasurable solitary pursuits, listen to our favorite music, ride our Harley, go swimming, golfing, watch TV, and so on.

Case study:

Becky's aunt had just gotten off the plane from Spain. She had traveled to Michigan in order to help celebrate her niece's Bat Mitzvah later that night. Before she could get through Customs, she had a massive heart attack and died.

Becky and her family were devastated. Her family faced a difficult decision: go on with the service and celebration or postpone them in order to mourn her aunt's death.

Becky and her parents had been planning her Bat Mitzvah for four years; she had attended Hebrew school to learn how to read Hebrew and chant from the Torah. Preparations for her celebration had been in the works for the past year – the hall, food, music, and decorations were all paid for. Other family members and friends had come in from out of town.

With the help of their rabbi, Becky's family decided to follow through with their original plans while still recognizing their loss. It was difficult, but the clergy and the congregation supported Becky and her family. There were moments of sadness, but also moments of happiness during the service that night and the celebration that followed the next day.

# ~ 18 ~

> Simona Sez . . .
>
> "It is important to be congruent."

To ensure good mental health, we must be able to integrate our thoughts, feelings, and experiences. If unable to do so, psychopathology can develop.

Case study:

One thirty-year-old patient had always been criticized for expressing her feelings. As a child, she was told to stop her stupid laughter, and asked, "What in the world are you crying about NOW?" By the time she entered treatment, she had learned to repress her feelings so she would not be criticized for them. Since she was overweight, it was apparent that she also "stuffed" herself with food, leaving no room for her to experience her feelings.

In treatment, she first had to learn how to recognize that she was having feelings and then to identify what particular feeling she was experiencing. Next, she needed to connect these feelings with her thoughts and experiences. We worked on detangling incongruent thoughts and feelings and understanding where they came from. This work enabled her to make decisions about her life based on accurate information.

## Simona Sez . . .

"All that we are today is a product of all we have been in our lifetimes."

From the moment of birth, through our relationship with others and our environment, we gather experiences that contribute to our personalities. Positive and negative experiences combine to create our totality.

Case study:

Monica was raised in a poor and chaotic household. Her father was verbally abusive while drunk. His mantra to his children was, "You expletive, expletive kids should have never been born! You'd all be better off dead!" As if that were not enough, Monica's mother often times told her to go play in traffic. Monica grew up feeling worthless and depressed. She often contemplated suicide.

In therapy, Monica came to understand her parents' statements were reflections of their pathology based on their childhoods - not a reflection of her.

She realized her painful experiences as a child had laid the foundation for her to be a very compassionate person, one who was able to give to others and always side with the underdog! This awareness boosted Monica's self-esteem and helped lift the veil of depression she had worn most of her life.

During one therapy session, Monica proudly proclaimed, "I am happy I was born! And I am happy to be alive!"

Through the course of her treatment, Monica learned to first trust me, then herself, and then others. She not only gave to others; now she was able to accept what others gave her. Based on our relationship, she developed the ability to engage in emotionally intimate relationships.

Simona Sez . . .

"If we want things to be different, WE have to MAKE them be different!"

People are often propelled into therapy due to unhappiness in a relationship. Occasionally the individual realizes that he or she has issues that contribute to the problems in the relationship and that *he or she* needs to change.* Amazingly, though, some people continue to engage in their usual behavior and expect the other person in the relationship to change and then wonder why everything stays the same.

*Change requires us to actively engage in new behavior.

Case study:

Chandra, a middle-aged divorcée, entered therapy stating that she was depressed and stressed out. She attributed her depression and stress to her teenage daughters, who she said were treating her disrespectfully. As we explored her concerns, it became clear that the demarcation in their behavior coincided with the onset of a new love relationship for Chandra in which she began using drugs in front of her daughters and leaving them unsupervised for entire weekends at a time. Now seeing the whole picture, Chandra realized that she had to take responsibility for her actions in order to alleviate her depression and stress.

~ 24 ~

> Simona Sez . . .
>
> "Experiencing our issues is the best teacher."

Frustration is common when dealing with someone who pushes our buttons. During and following these encounters, we are flooded with thoughts and feelings. While this is extremely uncomfortable, these experiences provide a forum for us to learn to deal with our issues and thus can be viewed as a tool for change.

Case study:

During a brainstorming meeting at work, Randy shared his idea for a new project. When his manager openly criticized him, Randy shut down.

At his next therapy session, Randy shared that, while growing up, his family was always very critical of him. When he did not share their views or feelings on an issue, they expressed their disapproval. After these situations, he would go to his room to be by himself. While hurt and angry, he also felt bad about himself. He felt like there was something wrong with him. These interactions and their sequella contributed to his depression and low self-esteem.

Randy agreed with my interpretation that his parents were filled with anxiety and could not tolerate any differentness – not that he was wrong, bad, or stupid. He could now comprehend the possibility of people holding different views and feelings and still maintaining mutual respect. In the end, Randy was thankful that his manager had given him the opportunity to examine these issues.

> Simona Sez . . .
>
> "Some opportunities come disguised as problems."

None of us literally stand in line waiting for problems to be handed out to us. To extrapolate further, no one *should* go looking for problems. However, being presented with problems helps us discover our strengths and our weaknesses, thereby giving us an opportunity to grow.

Case study:

Ralph began one therapy session by sharing the upset he had felt with one of his coworkers earlier that day. He said he had been having a seemingly pleasant conversation when one coworker began making racially denigrating remarks about another employee in the company.

Ralph had heard these types of remarks from others in the past and had always wanted to admonish the people who said them. Drawing on his strengths, Ralph told his colleague that his racially disparaging remarks were unacceptable. Further conversation ensued. When the discussion ended, Ralph felt a sense of pride for living his values and using his voice to stand up for a coworker.

> Simona Sez . . .
>
> "Memories of traumatic experiences are never as bad as the experiences themselves."

People entering therapy frequently express fear about uncovering traumatic childhood experiences as the result of being in therapy.

When we experience trauma, our first instinct is to tell other people about it. We want to talk about what we saw, experienced, and felt before, during, and after the trauma occurred. During childhood, however, we are often silenced by the adults in our lives who do not want to deal with our pain. Therapy provides an opportunity to talk about trauma in a safe, non-judgmental environment.

Case study:

At age nine, Blair witnessed a fatal school bus accident as she rode another school bus home. Her prolonged ride was filled with anxiety, fear, and sadness. Blair arrived home to a house full of company, and, while there was a cursory mention of the accident, her parents' attention quickly shifted back to their guests.

Blair went to her room alone. She tried not to remember what she had seen, heard, and felt as a result of the accident; after all, if her parents would not let her talk about it, maybe it was too awful to even think about! The accident was never spoken about again until Blair was months into her therapy.

In therapy, Blair was encouraged to tell the "whole story" of the bus accident – the minutes before hand, the accident itself, accompanied by all the sights and sounds, her thoughts and feelings, her attempts to tell her parents about what happened, being alone with it in her room that night, and what all of it meant to her. While initially apprehensive about the feelings that might arise in telling the story, Blair said afterwards that she felt a sense of relief because she was no longer alone with the memories of her experience.

> Simona Sez . . .
>
> "Life presents us with many choices."

"Let's Make a Deal" was a television game show created in the 1960s. Its premise is a good example of the choices we have in life. In this game, contestants were able to decide whether they wanted the prize behind door number one, door number two, or door number three. Of course, they did not know what was behind each door, and, while some of the prizes were valuable, some of them were simply funny.

Case study:

Early in my career, I worked with a 35-year-old woman who had recently married for the third time. Husband number three was just like Rose's previous spouses: physically, emotionally, and verbally abusive. Exploration revealed that the pattern of abuse had been set in childhood, with Rose's father the initial perpetrator.

During her second appointment, Rose spoke in detail about the abuse she had suffered just the night before. Through her sobs, Rose said she felt she could no longer tolerate it. She confided, "I'm either going to run away, go crazy, or kill myself."

Within a heartbeat, I said, "It sounds like you feel you have a choice." As we talked, Rose said that women in her family typically had "nervous breakdowns" (i.e., had become psychotic) when faced with the same level of stress she was experiencing now. As a result of our discussion, she realized that she did have a choice and therefore could consider healthier options. That night, Rose entered a shelter for battered women.

Simona Sez . . .

"A crisis can help us jump-start the process of change."

Most of us do not seek crises, although there are some who grew up in chaotic homes and choose professions that inherently provide chaos.

Most of us travel through life down familiar paths in a ritualistic manner. As long as everything remains the same, we remain the same. A crisis, however, can jolt us into realizing that something in our lives is not working for us and that we need to make changes.

Case study:

When Rebecca's husband moved out of their marital home and told her he was filing for divorce, she quickly called for a psychotherapy evaluation. While shocked and hurt, she wasn't *really* surprised. She shared that she had shut her husband out of her life many years ago and also acknowledged drinking on a daily basis for the past ten years.

Spurred on by this crisis, Rebecca could now admit to being an alcoholic. She joined Alcoholics Anonymous, where she made a pledge to be abstinent and a commitment to change. Therapy and AA meetings encouraged Rebecca to be open with others and to let others into her life.

The crisis initiated by her husband's moving out enabled Rebecca to assess her life and make the changes needed so she would not continue to be an alcoholic who was emotionally alone in the world.

> Simona Sez . . .
>
> "We must understand where we have come from in order to emotionally grow beyond where we are today."

As we reflect on our pasts, it is helpful to recognize patterns developed over our lifetimes. Some are helpful to us and some are not. In order to change, we must understand how and why these dynamics evolved. By doing so, we can consciously work on being different.

Case study:

Kelly was born into a family of very strong matriarchal women. Her mother was domineering, controlling, and codependent. Kelly's attempts to express her individuality were met with silent anger, and her expressions of her thoughts and feelings fell on deaf ears. When she experienced any difficulties in her life, she was left to deal with them by herself.

Her parents did acknowledge Kelly's achievements: her straight A's in school, her presidency of the student council, her being captain of the cheerleading team, and so on. As an adult, Kelly became an overachiever in business, controlling a lot of people and a lot of things. She was loved by her employees, who she "coached" to prepare for promotions.

All the while, Kelly did not take care of herself; she was out of control in regard to her weight, finances, and clutter! Therapy helped Kelly understand that she had identified with her mother and that her experience of living for other people's expectations and pleasure had jeopardized her own life. This insight allowed Kelly to begin taking steps to take better care of herself.

Simona Sez . . .

"Balance is an essential ingredient in life."

Take a moment to think about someone you know who is an alcoholic, a workaholic, a shopaholic, or a foodaholic. You will notice that that person's life is "consumed" by their habit. Any time a person limits themselves to engaging in just one or two behaviors, their life is out of balance.

Case study:

Leonard was a workaholic. He awoke early each day to arrive at the office by 7 AM and would not return home until after 8 PM. On top of the long hours he spent at the office, he took work home with him. Leonard rationalized that this was the only way he could earn a promotion. Frequent business trips, eating at his desk, and his lack of exercise all added to Leonard's inherited issues of high cholesterol and heart problems.

The day Leonard began having severe chest pain and was rushed to the emergency room by ambulance was the day he started to realize that the scales of his life were tipped out of balance. After his triple bypass surgery, Leonard began doing cardiovascular exercises, improved his diet, cut back on his work hours, and entered psychotherapy.

> Simona Sez . . .
>
> "It's important to try on lots of hats – otherwise we won't know what style, fabric, or color fits us best."

What style of hat fits you best? What fabric is the most comfortable for you? What color hat looks best on you? Here are just a few examples of the different types of hats that are available: balmoral, baseball, beanie, beret, straw, cowboy, fedora, fez, panama, top hat, and trilby hat. Sometimes we try on one type, fabric, and color of hat and feel satisfied that we have found the right one for us - only to find out later that there is yet another hat that is a better fit for us.

Case study:

From the age of five, I knew I wanted to be a practical nurse when I grew up, just like my mom. At sixteen, I became a Candy Striper at a local hospital. In high school, I took all the medical classes offered and became a co-op nurse assistant when I was a senior.

After high school, I went to nursing school and became a licensed practical nurse. However, as soon I started practicing as an LPN, I discovered I did not like *working* as a nurse even though I liked *being* a nurse.

For me, the best part of being a nurse was offering patients emotional support and providing an opportunity for them to talk about their hospitalization or illness. Unfortunately, time was usually not available to engage in listening and I found that my nurse's cap did not fit as well as I had thought it would.

I soon went back to college and graduated first with my Bachelor's Degree in Social Work and then with my Master's Degree in Social Work. Thirty plus years later, I can tell you that my social work hat fits me to a T.

My story is not unique.

Sometimes it is a career hat that needs changing; sometimes it's a relationship or an aspect of ourselves that we have outgrown.

Regardless of the reason, we need to try on multiple "hats" in our lifetimes in order to find the one that fits us best.

> Simona Sez . . .
>
> "Behind the clouds, the sun is shining!"

I traveled solo when I took my first plane trip at the age of sixteen. It was a completely overcast, very cold Michigan day in December 1967 when I boarded and took my window seat. Excited and nervous, I kept my eyes wide open and fixed on the happenings outside the window. To my surprise and delight, as the plane climbed toward the sky and broke through the clouds, I saw the sun shining brightly.

Case study:

At that moment, I "got" it. I understood that even when clouds are their darkest, when we are faced with the greatest difficulties, something positive *can* evolve.

My mother died four months later. I was devastated. As a seventeen-year-old, I was still searching for my identity and gaining independence. Although I had a lot to learn, I knew that my life would never be the same again.

From the devastation of my mother's death, and the darkness of my grief, I developed an understanding of the process of loss and grief. As a result, I have spent much of my professional life as a clinical social worker, helping others who have also experienced loss in their lives.

Simona Sez . . .

"We are in control of our own lives even when we behave out of control. In other words, we are in control - of being out of control."

We consciously make a choice when we decide to eat our third brownie, drink the extra martini, or put the pedal to the metal to speed.

Case study:

Dane always knew when he was going to lose his temper. It happened every time someone said no to him. Dane did not like to be told *no*.

Whenever someone said no to him, Dane would find a way to get them to say yes. He would start by raising his voice. If that did not work, he would begin yelling and screaming. If need be, Dane would continue to escalate into a full rage until the other person gave in.

Amazingly, Dane always deescalated the moment he heard the word *yes*.

> Simona Sez . . .
>
> "We cannot change where we come from, but we *can* change the moment we are in, and, hence, change the complexion of our future."

At some point in our lives, we may become aware of something about ourselves that we wish to change. Rather than berating ourselves for past thoughts, feelings, or behaviors, it is important to gain insight into the reasons we have been that particular way and then to accept our decisions and experiences up until that time. From that moment on, though, we can do everything necessary to change our perspective, our behavior, and, ultimately, our experience. As we engage in the process of change, we reshape the trajectory of our future.

Case study:

As noted in the last example, Dane had an anger management problem. His temper had created problems in relationships for years, but Dane chose not to examine his behavior until he lost his job after going into a rage at work. Dane felt ashamed of his behavior and was angry with himself for allowing his anger to escalate at work.

In therapy, Dane began to explore the roots of his anger issues. He was never allowed to discuss his feelings at home; his father pent up his feelings until he exploded. Dane had no one to turn to for comfort and had not learned how to be compassionate with himself, either. Therapy taught Dane to recognize and express his thoughts and feelings in a safe manner. He learned to be compassionate with himself and how to soothe himself when he was upset.

> Simona Sez . . .
>
> "Integrity means living your values and being honest with yourself as well as others."

I have counseled many people who recognize the importance of living a life of integrity. As they talk about the concept, it is clear that they are referring to how they communicate with others – i.e., they pride themselves on being honest in their dealings and relationships with others.

What is suspiciously missing, though, is their honesty and integrity with themselves. For example, they set personal goals and objectives and then fail to follow through, as many do with their New Year's resolutions. Under these circumstances, people end up feeling disappointed and angry with themselves and then continue engaging in the behavior that they wanted to change.

Case study:

Derrick valued keeping physically fit. In his 20s, he prepared for and ran in many marathons. In his 30s, however, he spent much of his time as a couch potato, either watching TV or reading. He felt contempt for himself for not spending more time engaging in physical activity.

In order to effect change, Derrick needed to understand the incongruence between what he valued and how he chose to live his life. Furthermore, Derrick needed help to realize that he had not been honest with himself, a trait he valued in his relationships with others.

# II.

# Family & Relationships

> **Create a home that will provide the opportunity for refueling.**

> **Simona Sez . . .**
>
> "Home is where we go for refueling."

Our homes are our refuge. They are where we go to get away from the demands of the rest of the world. When our home lives allow us to refuel, we recharge our emotional batteries and gain the strength necessary to go back out into the world.

For someone who lives alone, the home should be clean and uncluttered, a place where the resident can nurture him- or herself with healthy foods and favorite activities. It is also a place where family and friends can gather together for relaxation, good conversation, and entertainment.

When living with others, the same parameters are required. In addition, though, the home must be one in which all members can be refueled; this home is filled with love, mutual respect, trust, acceptance, understanding, compassion, privacy, and cooperation. While no individual and no family is able to provide this for its members a hundred percent of the time, it is important to approximate this loving behavior the majority of the time so that each member in the home has a chance to be refueled.

Case study:

Renee, a university senior and commuter who lived with her family, was preparing to take the LSATs. There were healthy meals for Renee to eat and her home was quiet so she could study. Renee's younger sister and brother, also college students, were great listeners when Renee wanted to talk about the stress she was experiencing. Family members assumed Renee's responsibilities so she could devote her time to studying, relaxing, or taking good care of herself. Although stressed, Renee was refueled at home and able to deal with the pressure. Due in no small part to the support she received at home, Renee passed her LSATs and was accepted into law school.

Case study:

April 15$^{th}$, income tax day, was a month away. Jay, a CPA, had a large caseload and was spending a lot of time at the office completing his clients' tax forms. There were a lot of demands on him.

At home, Jay's wife was complaining about the time he put in at the office and about the problems she was having with their children. Jay's seventeen-year-old son had been taking his younger sister's laptop against her wishes. The television was on incessantly. All of the fighting in the home created extra tension.

When Jay was next able to get away from the office, he went to the bar instead of going home – at least at the bar, he thought, the bartender would listen to his tales of woe and he could relax with a beer.

> Simona Sez . . .
>
> "An intimate conversation is better than an orgasm."

Think about the deep conversations you have had with others, conversations in which there was a deep level of vulnerability and mutual understanding. The good feelings that arise from these types of conversations can last for days, whereas the good feelings from an orgasm generally last for only moments.

Consider this: The therapeutic dyad is composed of transference, countertransference, and a real relationship. Shifting between these relationships at any given moment allows the therapist and patient to mimic the dancing of a waltz. The flow between the two is harmonious – the same waltz that occurs in our everyday emotionally intimate relationships.

Case study:

Twenty-five-year-old Jackie had been in weekly therapy for a few months when she suddenly asked this question one session: "Are you not interested in working with me?" When I inquired, Jackie said that she had seen me look at the clock and had interpreted this action to mean that I was uninterested in working with her.

Further exploration revealed that Jackie's parents had raised her with a laissez-faire attitude. She had no set bedtime, no bedtime rituals, no requests to brush her teeth, bathe, or wear a jacket in winter. Jackie grew up feeling unloved and unlovable.

She transferred these feelings to me, as her therapist, and searched for behavior on my part that would confirm her beliefs. When she saw me look at the clock, Jackie felt she had all the evidence she needed to assure herself that I was just like her parents. Unlike her parents, however, I sought to understand Jackie's reaction, thereby dispelling her fears and deepening our conversation.

The closeness between us was palpable that hour. Feeling understood permitted Jackie to experience the beginning of a new type of relationship – a safe one in which all things are talkable. The trust developed during this session paved the way to a deep relationship between us in which Jackie was able to work through her past and current issues.

Simona Sez...

"What really matters *is* what really matters."

Sometimes we are fooled into believing that having expensive clothes, the latest technological gadgets, and popular cars is what's really important.

Remembering that we really have nothing if we don't have our health and that life is much sweeter with the love and companionship of family and friends reminds us that material possessions matter less than the things that are truly important: our health, family, and friends.

Case study:

Janine liked nice things, especially jewelry that sparkled. She went into enormous debt after years of purchases on cable's QVC. She began working a second job in order to pay down her debt. As a result, she had less time to sleep, her eating habits worsened, and her health suffered.

Janine eventually experienced panic attacks and went to the emergency room when she thought she was having a heart attack. When all of her tests revealed no physical abnormalities, the doctor in the emergency room recommended psychotherapy. In therapy, Janine came to understand that her jewelry purchases had a twofold purpose: to allow her to experience instant gratification and to quell the emptiness she felt inside.

Therapy helped Janine identify the roots of her feelings of emptiness, to grieve for what she had missed in childhood, and to learn to take care of herself.

Simona Sez . . .

"That which we don't put into words, we put into action."

One law of physics states that energy is neither created nor destroyed - it just changes form.

Case study:

During a heated marital session, Mark interrupted Betsy several times in order to explain his side of the issue. Each time he did, Betsy took a small deep breath and allowed Mark to continue. When Mark interrupted a fourth time, Betsy said sarcastically, "And I never liked the necklace you bought me for my birthday!"

As we examined their interaction, Betsy was able to talk about how hurt she felt each time Mark talked over her – as if, she said, what she had to say was unimportant. She kept quiet, though, because she did not want things to escalate into an all-out fight. Examining this interaction allowed Mark and Betsy to realize that Betsy's decision to keep quiet about her hurt feelings only meant they would surface in another manner; in this case, Betsy made a sarcastic comment about a gift Mark gave her, intending to repay Mark for hurting her.

> Simona Sez . . .
>
> "Everyone needs a voice."

Parents in the 1950s and 1960s often told their children that they were "meant to be seen and not heard," a saying that many of those children took to heart.

Some adults in therapy share their experiences of being ignored, ridiculed, or shamed if they expressed their thoughts or feelings, in words or behavior, while growing up. One woman in therapy frequently used the expression, "For crying out loud," as if crying loudly was the only way to get someone's attention in order to be 'heard.'

Case study:

Rose, a septuagenarian, entered therapy due to stress and difficulty getting a restful night's sleep. During her wakeful hours, she tried to keep busy to fend off any uncomfortable thoughts or feelings. At bedtime, her mind was flooded with all of the issues that she had tried to avoid during the day.

During our exploration, Rose shared that she rarely expressed her thoughts or feelings to others, whether about her own concerns or their behavior toward her. In time, she came to understand that her silence was directly responsible for her stress and restless sleep.

As we examined the barriers to her using her voice, we noted there were many, including this message given to her decades before: "If you don't have something nice to say, don't say anything at all."

With this understanding, Rose decided she had been silent too long. As she started to use her voice, she was a little frightened of how forceful she could be. Time and experience helped her learn to express herself in an assertive manner. One session, after reporting a successful interaction with a friend, Rose proudly announced, "I have a voice!"

Simona Sez . . .

"We do not have a ticker tape that runs across our foreheads to let others know what we are thinking, feeling, or experiencing. If we want someone else to know what is going on inside of us, we need to share it with them."

There seems to be a misunderstanding, especially among couples, that each of the partners knows exactly what the other is thinking, feeling, or experiencing without the other person ever verbalizing it. Problems ensue when we behave as if these assumptions are correct.

Case study:

Marianne reported sitting quietly on the couch enjoying a book one Saturday morning while her husband John sat in his favorite chair watching the news. Seemingly out of nowhere, John stormed out of the room. They ended up spending the day apart.

In a joint session, Marianne shared her confusion about their interaction; she was quietly reading her book when John stormed out of the room. John explained that he had become anxious with the quietness between them. Further exploration revealed that while he was growing up his mother gave him the silent treatment when she was angry with him. Based on his history, John had assumed that Marianne was angry with him. Instead of talking with her about it, he had acted on his assumption.

> Simona Sez . . .
>
> "Despite our wishes to control people, places, and things, we really only have control over our own behavior,; and sometimes we don't even have that."

Everyone has heard someone say how much better their life would be "if only" __ __ __ (fill in the blanks) would __ __ __ (fill in the blanks).

To highlight the concept of powerlessness, try to <u>make</u> the sun shine if it is a cloudy day, or <u>make</u> the day warmer if it is a little chilly. IMPOSSIBLE! Now, concentrate on the things that you *can* change.

Case study:

Joann began dating soon after her divorce. During her initial appointment, she said she had found the "man of her dreams" in her relationship with Stan. She went on to say that it would be the most perfect relationship, *"if only"* Stan was more supportive. When asked what she meant, she said that Stan usually tuned her out, tried to minimize her concerns, or solve her problems when she shared her feelings.

She had tried to <u>make</u> Stan the perfect man by purchasing self-help books and reading them together, by confronting him about his dismissive behavior, by bribing him, and by threatening to end their relationship.

Two months into her therapy, Joann revealed that she had been drinking four martinis every night for years. As we explored this, Joann was able to understand that the only way to have a good relationship was to take good care of herself first - she needed to quit drinking and begin a recovery program. Although Joann's relationship with Stan eventually ended, she could see how expecting Stan to change prevented her from looking at her own behavior.

## Simona Sez . . .

"It's unrelated to you."

We all carry our best and worst with us wherever we go, so we can easily become entangled in other people's pathology.

Case study:

Matt's friend laughed at him one day when he admitted that he was afraid of flying. This interaction catapulted Matt into feelings of humiliation, anxiety, depression, and self-doubt. Though shaking inside and wanting to defend himself, Matt walked away silently.

In discussing his "friend," Matt revealed that John frequently laughed at other people's expense and made others the butt of his jokes. It appeared that John was a very insecure man who needed to put others down in order to elevate himself - the bully syndrome.

Matt also shared that, while growing up, his family teased him whenever he expressed his fears. He was, after all, supposed to be a "little man" and not be afraid. As an adult, whenever he was laughed at, Matt would become hooked and again experience all the upset first felt as a child.

In time, Matt understood that he became hooked in the present because of his past experiences. He could now separate his own issues from others' issues and thereby disentangle from them, averting a downward spiral of feelings.

Simona Sez . . .

"Your words say one thing — but your behavior says another."

Saying one thing and behaving in a contradictory way occurs quite frequently. The reason: we may be trying to hide how we feel; we may not be aware that we think one way and yet feel very differently; or it may be due to unconscious processes.

Case study:

Tony said he wanted to get married. He had dated Haley for years and recently asked for her hand in marriage. They set a date to marry and began all the prenuptial planning.

By law, it was required that they obtain a marriage license from the State of Michigan a minimum of three days prior to the wedding – which Tony failed to do.

In exploring the incongruity between Tony's words and his behavior, it became clear that Tony did not want to get married. While he loved his fiancée, he was not ready for marriage. He admitted to succumbing to the pressure of family and friends, who convinced him it was time for him to "settle down" and start a family.

> Simona Sez . . .
>
> "Sometimes we see what we think we see."

There are at least two sides to every story. And then there is this maxim: There are three sides to every story. His side, her side, and the truth.

Case study:

Cathy and Jason entered therapy to deal with their troubled marriage. Cathy had been having an extramarital affair because she did not feel Jason was meeting her emotional needs. While Jason was devastated by Cathy's infidelity, he saw it as a wakeup call and was eager to repair their marriage. At the same time, though, Jason was understandably leery about trusting Cathy and was always on the lookout for new evidence of Cathy's unfaithfulness.

The couple began one session talking about an incident that occurred at a party they had attended over the weekend. Jason had suspected that Cathy was interested in one of the men at the party, so he had watched her very closely. When Jason witnessed Cathy don a pair of "cheaters," he became very upset and insisted they leave the party. They did not speak again until their session.

Cathy explained that she had put on the glasses in order to read something she was handed, while Jason insisted she put them on to get a better view of the handsome man, who had been outside with some other guests.

Convinced that he knew what he saw, it took the full session for Jason to understand that "cheaters" are glasses used to help people read what is in front of them and that anything in the distance would be blurred, not made clearer!

Simona Sez . . .

"Different people are ready for different things at different times."

Some patients express disappointment in themselves for not completely understanding their issues on their own or for not entering therapy to deal with their issues at an earlier time.

Case study:

One day at work, Eric became so angry that he banged his fist on his desk loudly enough to frighten other employees in his vicinity. Eric's supervisor was called and Eric was escorted to his boss's office. Eric was given two weeks of unpaid time off. Upon returning to work two weeks later, Eric was told he was demoted, and that, as a condition of employment, he had to attend anger management therapy.

Eric had always had problems with his temper. He had screaming matches with his wife on a regular basis. He said things to her that he felt shame for afterwards. And while this created upheavals in his marriage, eventually things would settle down, Eric would apologize to his wife, and life would continue as usual.

In therapy, Eric expressed disappointment with himself for having let his anger get the best of him and for not having dealt with it appropriately prior to his acting out at work and being demoted. In this case, it was the consequence of Eric's acting out behavior that enabled him to be ready to confront his life time struggle with his unresolved anger.

> Simona Sez . . .
>
> "Oftentimes we say things or behave in ways that we regret afterwards."

Sometimes we say or do things that are childish, hurtful, angry, or malicious – and this is not an inclusive list! While we cannot take our words or behaviors back, we have an opportunity to apologize. In our apologies, we can let the other person know we are unhappy with our behavior and explain how we would do it differently if we had the chance to do it over again.

Case study:

Angela was hurt when Ryan worked overtime to finish a project instead of coming home so the two of them could go to dinner together as planned.

When Ryan finally arrived home, Angela said, "I am so disappointed that we did not go to dinner together. I was really looking forward to having that special time with you."

Ryan replied, "I'm sorry for hurting your feelings; I can hear it was important to you that we spend that time together. May I have a do-over?"

"Yes."

Ryan went on, "If I could do it over, I would meet you for dinner as planned, and then go back to the office to finish working on my project."

Angela smiled. "I accept your apology. I feel that you understand why I was disappointed and that, given the same circumstances again, the outcome would be different."

> Simona Sez . . .
>
> "Emotional strength is the direct result of being emotionally vulnerable!"

Being emotionally strong is sometimes interpreted as keeping one's feelings to oneself. Being told not to "cry like a baby," to "buck up," and to "take it like a man" are the types of messages one might hear while growing up. Viewing it from this perspective, it is easy to understand how one could come to feel that the expression of feelings would indicate weakness.

However, it is by allowing ourselves to be emotionally vulnerable with people we trust that we can gain emotional strength.

Case study:

In therapy, Mary asserted that she needed to be strong. She avoided topics that might create sadness and the filling of her eyes with tears. She was sure that I would criticize her, not like her, or terminate her therapy if she revealed how "weak" she was.

"What are you crying about now?" and "Stop that stupid laughter!" were messages Mary often heard while growing up. Mary interpreted these messages as meaning she should not express her feelings – either in behavior *or* word. In time, Mary learned to go off by herself and cry when her feelings consumed her.

After many months of dabbling in talk about her feelings during sessions, Mary began to trust me and allow herself to be more open. As this process continued, Mary started feeling better about herself. She continued to gain confidence and recognized that, in revealing her vulnerability, she had become emotionally stronger.

> ## Simona Sez...
>
> "Communication is more than the sending of a message. It also involves the 'receiver' receiving the message as it was intended."

Recall the game of "Telephone" from childhood: A group of children sit in a circle. One child whispers something in the ear of the child sitting next to him or her. The second child repeats the message to the third child. This continues until the last child in the circle has heard the message.

Once the last child receives the message, that child repeats the message out loud. Much laughter ensues when the children hear how different the message is after it has been passed from child to child. In most cases, the last child does not receive the same message whispered by the first child.

Using someone else as a conduit for your communication often alters your message. A variety of factors related to the receiver of the message can also alter reception of communication. For example, the receiver may be tired, engrossed in something else, or dealing with their own issues.

Case study:

As winter faded and the temperature began to climb, Ellen asked her husband to tune up her bike in preparation for the first nice day of spring. Peter agreed to do so. When that day arrived, and Ellen asked him if he'd had a chance to complete the work on her bike, Peter began yelling at Ellen and accused her of being angry with him for watching TV.

When they had a chance to look at their interaction, Peter said he had felt guilty when Ellen asked about her bike because he had not yet attended to it. Ellen had intentionally waited to ask Peter about her bike when there was a commercial on to avoid disrupting his baseball game. Ellen said she was happy that Peter was taking time to watch TV after having worked hard all week and that she was only wondering about the preparedness of her bike – she wanted to take it for a spin.

Simona Sez . . .

"Trusting others and being trusted requires 'reciprocated vulnerability.'"

Visualize a cat or dog, on its back, anxiously waiting to have its belly rubbed by a trusted individual. In human relationships, that type of trust shared by two people is considered reciprocated vulnerability.

Case study:

Kenneth and Nancy had been in previous relationships that had ended badly. Both showed evidence of emotional scars. Despite this, they both wanted their new relationship to succeed and were eager and willing to work on it.

Kenneth and Nancy entered relationship therapy. Their goal was to develop an emotionally intimate relationship with one another. They took turns being vulnerable, and, with each experience, they were rewarded with greater feelings of understanding, compassion, and trust for one another. In time, they developed an emotionally intimate relationship based on their ability to be open and honest with one another.

Simona Sez ...

"Beware of the person who is carrying a hot potato."

As kids, we used to play a game called hot potato. In this game, children standing in a circle toss an object that symbolizes a hot potato to each other while music plays. The hot potato is tossed quickly because, when the music stops, the child holding it is out of the game.

As adults, hot potato involves a person tossing their bad mood to someone else. The person who catches the bad mood then frequently tosses it on to someone else, and so on.

Case study:

Tom came in for his weekly appointment ready to talk about his horrible workday.

Tom's secretary, Laura, had been yelled at by her husband prior to leaving home that morning, so she started her work day in a very bad mood. All morning long, Tom found his reasonable requests answered with an attitude.

Eventually Tom caught Laura's "hot potato." By afternoon, Tom passed it on to Jim, snapping at his coworker when asked an innocent question about one of their joint projects.

> Simona Sez . . .
>
> "Don't invest in Enron."

In late 2001, a series of scandals involving irregular accounting procedures caused Enron Corporation's investors' equity to plummet from $85.00 to $0.30 per share.

In human interactions, not investing in Enron translates into not investing time and energy into a relationship with the hope of a high yield when it is obvious that the return on the investment will be negligible.

Case study:

Thirty-year-old Tiffany had a history of relationships with self-centered men beginning with her father. She consciously made an effort to choose a man who was the opposite of her dad but repeatedly failed. Each time she ended a relationship, she told herself that the next one would be different.

With her biological clock ticking, Tiffany entered therapy. Then she met Michael. At first, the relationship seemed fine. Michael was attentive and liked to buy her nice things. Several weeks into their relationship, problems began surfacing. During one session, Tiffany confided that on multiple occasions, when she expressed her feelings to Michael, he changed the subject. When she expressed feelings of hurt from his lack of empathy, he laughed at her.

Though sad about this insight, Tiffany knew she had another self-centered man in her life. She quickly ended the relationship, understanding that sharing her feelings and investing her trust in Michael would not pay any dividends. Instead, her return for her investment was emotional pain!

> Simona Sez . . .
>
> "Dysfunction breeds dysfunction."

This expression relates to the *nurture* in the nature verses nurture question. While physical illness and mental illness can be inherited genetically, dysfunction is passed down based on how we are or are not nurtured early in life.

Case study:

Kendra, now 26, was raised by her father for the first two years of her life. She explained that her father had been laid off prior to her birth and was unable to secure another job until she was two. Concerned about the family's financial security, her parents decided that her mother should look for work. She was able to secure a full-time job.

Kendra described her father as someone who was nervous and who did not feel good about himself. During the two years he provided the majority of Kendra's care, he watched her like a hawk. When she cried, he immediately ran to see what was "wrong." He didn't allow anyone else to hold Kendra because he didn't want them to pass their germs to her.

When Kendra entered therapy, she too was anxious and exhibited poor self-esteem. She was overly concerned about her health and frequently went to the doctor. She lived with her parents because she became very anxious contemplating living alone. She worked as a clerk at a local store making minimum wage and did not feel good about it. She wanted to attend college but felt she wasn't smart enough and would not do well. She hoped therapy would help her resolve these issues. It did!

Simona Sez . . .

"Some things we can change, but some things we cannot. We need to focus on changing the things we *can* change."

Case study:

Robert had planned to go to an Ivy League university since his freshman year in high school and excitedly applied to that university in the fall of his senior year. While his grades and extracurricular activities could have guaranteed him a spot, competition was brutal and Robert was declined admission.

Dreams dashed, Robert half-heartedly accepted admission to his second choice. Meanwhile, he spent a lot of time and energy trying to understand *why* he had been declined admission. When Robert realized he was stuck, he called for a psychotherapy evaluation.

In therapy, Robert shared his anger and hurt about not being accepted into the Ivy League university. It was clear that this was a loss of face for him, as well as a rejection, that triggered feelings of loss and rejection from years earlier.

When we explored these earlier experiences, Robert shared that his mom had walked out on his family when he was five – he had never heard from her again. Robert realized that the "Why?" questions he'd been asking about the university of his dreams were substitutions for his real concern: Why had his mother left him? As soon as Robert was able to attach his thoughts and feelings to this experience, he found the opportunity to grieve for the loss of his mother and the feelings of rejection her walking out had left him with.

As therapy terminated, Robert was able to begin to enthusiastically plan for his year ahead at college.

Simona Sez . . .

"You know you are engaging in co-dependent behavior when you agree to do something for someone else and then feel resentful about it."

Feeling resentful is a red flag that indicates that co-dependent behavior is taking place.

Case study:

Betty had looked forward to going to the symphony for months. Early in the evening, as she prepared to leave, her younger sister came over with her latest problem, and Betty chose to forgo the symphony and stay home so she could help her sister resolve her problem. Betty could feel the resentment building inside her as the clock ticked past the hour the concert was scheduled to begin.

In session, Betty readily acknowledged that she had sacrificed her own wishes for her sister's expressed need. She then revealed a history of this same type of behavior with others. In fact, she traced this behavior to early childhood and her relationship with her mother. Eager for her mother's love, she would stay home and take care of her mother while her siblings went out to play with their friends. Even as she recalled these early years, she could remember the upset she'd feel in the pit of her stomach.

The experience of missing the symphony paved the way for Betty to explore her co-dependency, her needs, and how she would address similar issues in the future.

> Simona Sez . . .
>
> "No one is as invested in your life as you are."

Evaluating feedback from others can be challenging. Others' perceptions or opinions of you are usually colored by their issues. Additionally, others have not lived your life and do not always have enough information to reach a valid conclusion.

Case study:

When Martin's wife was pregnant with their first child, the couple decided that Martin would quit his job and be the full-time caregiver when his wife returned to work following her maternity leave. This made sense for them, since Judy earned a higher income than Martin and they wanted their children to be raised by a parent.

Martin really enjoyed being a stay-at-home dad. He took his children to "Mom-Tot" classes, gymnastics and swimming lessons. When he was not busy with his children, Martin tended to his family's home with all the requisite responsibilities.

Martin was frequently teased by his "friends" because he lived such a "cushy" life. One acquaintance even called his wife a "sugar mama." While initially very upset by these remarks, Martin was able to evaluate the comments in the context of his life and understand that his friends were envious of him because he did not live with the demands and pressures of the typical nine-to-five work schedule.

> Simona Sez...
>
> "Respect means seeing ourselves and others as being equal, regardless of our differences."

I am fortunate because I have an education in nursing and social work. The combination of knowledge and experience gleaned from these professions has taught me how people are more alike than different.

As a nurse, I saw firsthand how illness, accidents, and death befall people of all ages, religions, races, genders, sexual orientations, developmental abilities and socio-economic statuses.

As a social worker, I have listened as the very young and the very old have talked about wanting and needing to be loved, to love another, to be heard, to be respected, to be included, and to have a purpose.

Our physical and emotional worlds influence each other. This is how we are similar.

We are different in regard to religion, race, ethnicity, socioeconomic status, age, gender, sexual orientation, abilities, as well as level and type of education.

Those differences don't make one group of people better or worse than any other group; differences add variety to life. By celebrating our differences and recognizing our similarities, respect can flourish.

Case study:

Janna, a precocious child, was talking and walking by the time she was nine months old and holding conversations with adults by eighteen months. She loved to play with her dolls and her "Speak and Say," a hand-held computer for children. By two and a half, Janna could spell her name. Janna easily engaged in parallel play with her preschool classmates. At home, she loved having books read to her. Mister Rogers' Neighborhood was her favorite television program.

In elementary school, Janna began excelling in all subjects, including math and science. As the tallest and smartest in her class, she was clearly "different." She had few friends and spent hours alone after school. By middle school, Janna was the subject of ridicule; her classmates could not understand how she could actually "like" math and science and so teased her mercilessly.

Years later, in therapy, Janna shared that much of her validation had come from watching Mr. Rogers – the kind older man's gentle voice had explained the types of thoughts and feelings children experienced in various scenarios, allowing Janna to understand her own inner life. And the foundation of her love of science and math came from Mr. Rogers' explanations of "how things work."

Janna also shared the pain of being ridiculed by her classmates beginning in middle school and continuing through high school. She did not understand why her classmates did not like her – she had the same needs to be loved, accepted, included, and respected as they did. Therapy helped Janna accept that, although her classmates treated her disrespectfully, she was worthy of respect.

> Simona Sez . . .
>
> "I have never met a parent who has stood over their baby's crib and said, 'How can I mess this kid up?'"

Mothers of all ages feel anxious when their offspring enter therapy because they expect the therapist to point a finger at them as *the* cause of their child's problems.

However, no one is given a qualification test prior to embarking on parenthood. Every father and mother brings his or her lifelong struggles into the parent–child relationship, where these issues are played out. Such issues include feelings of insecurity, fear of abandonment, and sibling rivalry, to name just a few.

Many patients enter therapy wanting to blame someone else for their problems. Parents are likely targets. And while there may have been many mistakes made during a person's formative years, I like to "understand" what happened rather than assign blame.

Of course, it is imperative to fully explore disappointments, hurts, and anger toward others, including parents. Following exploration, expression of feelings, and insight, acceptance often takes the place of blame. It is also important for people to accept that, regardless of the issues carried forward as a result of their childhoods, they alone are responsible for their decisions and behavior as adults.

Case study:

Monica's case on page 21 is a good example of how understanding the origins of a parent's behavior can allow acceptance to replace blame.

Monica's father was an alcoholic whose mantra was, "You expletive, expletive kids should have never been born! You'd all be better off dead!" Monica's mother often told her to go play in traffic. Monica grew up feeling worthless and depressed. She often contemplated suicide.

In therapy, Monica spent many months expressing profound hurt and intense anger toward her parents for being so cruel to her while she was growing up. Monica sometimes cried openly and sometimes raged as she shared her traumatic childhood experiences. Interspersed with stories of her own childhood, Monica shared stories of her grandparents.

Her paternal grandfather had died at a young age, leaving her father to be raised by his mother. Monica's paternal grandmother was a very critical and controlling woman who ended up being the sole provider and caretaker of the family farm.

Her maternal grandparents, Monica related, fled Poland as Hitler came to power in Germany. Living in a new country, being unable to speak English, and being responsible for earning a living overwhelmed her grandparents. Their time and patience were in short supply; Monica's mother received little nurturing.

Knowing and understanding that her parents' limitations were based on their childhoods allowed Monica to replace the anger and blame she had always felt for them with compassion.

# III.

# On Loss & Grief

In 1976, federal funding for Providence Hospital's drug abuse program was cut. As a result, I was transferred from the sixth floor of the hospital, where I had worked previously, to the basement, where both the Radiation Therapy and Oncology departments were housed. The patients who came to these departments were preparing for, receiving, or recovering from treatment for cancer. Most were pretty sick, though they didn't always know their diagnosis.

As a nurse, one of my responsibilities was to draw blood. Though drawing blood didn't take long, it still meant five minutes alone with each patient. During this time, some confided that their families were unaware that they knew their own diagnosis; these patients felt that they had no one to talk to about their experiences.

I felt really good that I was the kind of person others trusted with their secrets. I knew that my caring would make a difference in their lives even if I couldn't affect the outcome of their lives.

Many tried to dissuade me from working with cancer patients, including my mother-in-law, an Auschwitz survivor. They told me that it was too depressing to work with people with cancer because they would most likely die.

I never found it depressing.

I worked Radiation Therapy for the next year before returning to school full-time to pursue my social work degree. From 1981 to 1990, I volunteered with the American Cancer Society, where I facilitated a support group for cancer patients and their families called "Focus on Living."

I share this background because the next section may be difficult to read. There is nothing easy about loss and grief. But losses are real. And grief is a natural response to loss. Although the journey through the grief process is a very painful one, and one that no healthy person seeks out, it presents us with the opportunity to grow and learn healthy coping techniques for one of life's greatest challenges.

The experience of the grief that accompanies a loss is one of our most intense experiences; it is repeated over and over again in a myriad of ways throughout our lifetimes as a result of deaths, divorce, developmental changes, physical changes, relocation, job loss, social role loss . . . .

Loss is a universal experience. Beginning with the moment of birth, when the fetus is thrust from the safety, security, and familiarity of the mother's womb, and the umbilical cord is severed, and ending with the moment of death, we experience innumerable losses. Each of these losses is marked by a period of transition in which the individual attempts to integrate the loss and find an adaptive resolution to their new situation.

> Simona Sez . . .
>
> "When a loss occurs in the present, it sets off memories of past losses and ushers in fears of future losses."

Grief: Present, past, and future meld into one. A parent's death today may remind us of a grandparent's death years before and may be accompanied by fears of a spouse's death in the future. As we deal with a current loss, we have the opportunity to rework past losses and begin to prepare for future losses.

Case study:

Ten-year-old Andrea's father had recently died after a long battle with cancer. For the last two months of his life, hospice workers came to the house to care for Mr. Mason. Andrea knew her father was dying, as the hospice social worker facilitated that dialog between Andrea and her parents.

In the months following Mr. Mason's death, Andrea seemed anxious and depressed. Her grades plummeted. She wasn't interested in her usual activities. Her school counselor recommended therapy and a children's grief support group.

Through the pictures she drew during her therapy hour, Andrea shared her sadness about her father's and grandfather's deaths, as well as her anxiety that her mom might also get sick and die.

The grief Andrea felt about her father's death was intensified as a result of her grandfather's death two years prior. Fear of her mother's death was a natural progression of thought, as, at this point, two of the most important people in her life had died in the past two years.

Simona Sez . . .

"With multiple losses, we are like a fighter in the ring who has taken too many punches."

After an initial loss, we are like the fighter who comes into the ring ready to fight but gets punched so hard that he has a difficult time shaking off the blow. Eventually, the fighter is ready to fight again but is weaker than he was at the beginning of the match. When the next blow hits him, he falls to the mat and struggles to get up. On the count of seven, he is dazed but on his feet. If the fighter is dealt yet another blow, the referee will finish the count before the fighter can get to his feet again.

Case study:

Amber's 65-year-old mother died in January of 2006. They had had a wonderful relationship and Amber was devastated by her mom's death. Amber attended a grief support group offered by her church and was working through her grief when her sister died in a motor vehicle accident in December of the same year.

Amber's grief was now compounded. As a result of these multiple losses, timed so closely together, Amber experienced severe depression and was having difficulty functioning on a day-to-day basis, though she did try to put one foot in front of the other. During her yearly physical, she discussed this with her family practitioner, who advised her to seek therapy.

> Simona Sez . . .
>
> "The philosophy 'Time heals all wounds' does not apply to grief. It is not the time, per se, but what is done with the time!"

The passage of time alone will not heal the wounds left by the loss of a loved one. One must grieve fully. This includes experiencing the initial shock; the physical, emotional, psychological, mental, intellectual, and behavioral expressions that occur with grief; and the acceptance of the loss. One's ability to succeed in doing this "grief work" is influenced by the mourner's personality, past experiences with grief, the extent the loss affects everyday life, and the support available.

Case study:

Joan attended a grief support group after her husband died. She also talked with her family and friends about Bill: her missing him, how hard it was to go home to an empty house at night, and how she would sleep with his undershirt, which still had his scent on it. Joan talked about all aspects of her relationship with Bill, including the joys and struggles they had shared. Holidays were especially hard for Joan, but everyone respected her need to talk about Bill and grieve for his absence.

For Joan, time did heal the wounds of her loss, because she used her time to grieve well!

> Simona Sez . . .
>
> "Take an active part in working through your grief. It is not a passive process!"

You can:
-Familiarize yourself with the normal reactions of grief.
-Identify your thoughts, feelings, and behaviors as you experience them.
-Sensitize yourself to the many types of loss that may initiate a grief response.
-Surround yourself with people sensitive to you and your loss.
-Share your story through journaling or talking with others.
-Join a bereavement support group.

Case study:

Soon after her husband's death, Sandy began attending a bereavement support group. She wanted to be with other women whose husbands had died, feeling they might best understand what she was experiencing. She did not want anyone to judge her or try to squelch her crying or expressions of grief.

Sandy also created a scrapbook about her husband, his life, and their life together, as well as his death. It was not easy to do this, but Sandy felt it was therapeutic for her. In taking an active role in working through her grief, Sandy was able to come to terms with husband's death and start a new chapter in her life.

> Simona Sez ...
>
> "Embrace the pain of grief. Work, exercise, and respite need to be alternated with experiencing the pain of grief. A healthy balance will energize you and give you the strength you need to go on."

Grief is a normal response to any loss. Embracing grief allows you to fully experience the meaning of your loss so that you can accept it—keep in mind that acceptance <u>does not</u> mean you will like it! Without acceptance, your grief will go unresolved. Unresolved grief can lead to physical or mental illness.

Case study:

Jonathon was a workaholic prior to his wife's death and continued this behavior after Rona's death. He had always used work as a mechanism to avoid dealing with his internal life, and he thought this served him well after Rona died, too. Two years later, he was taken from his office to the hospital by ambulance; he had suffered a major heart attack. He was lucky. He survived.

When he completed cardiac rehabilitation, he began psychotherapy for emotional rehabilitation.

> Simona Sez . . .
>
> "There is often a 'domino' effect with a loss."

When a loved one dies, there are more losses than that of the individual who died because each person generally fills multiple roles.

For example: If the loss is of a spouse, the surviving partner may have lost their best friend; their lover; a second parent to their children; a homemaker; a breadwinner; a euchre partner; a golf partner; and the list goes on.

Case study:

Brenda's husband died after 32 years of marriage. She had spent all of her adult life with Andrew. He had been her spouse, best friend, cheering squad, intellectual companion, travel partner, and ray of sunshine. As Brenda spoke about Andrew and her life with him, she realized that Andrew had filled so many of her needs. She wondered how she would manage life without him.

> Simona Sez . . .
>
> "We cannot 'get over' the death of a loved one."

Unlike the flu or a cold, the death of a loved one is *never* something you can "get over." After a loved one dies, your life will never be the same. However, if you grieve well, you will be able to come to accept your loved one's death and begin a new chapter of your life. This is a process which takes time and work to achieve.

Case study:

Catherine and Ralph dated for two years prior to their marriage, which spanned 43 years. Upon Ralph's death, Catherine took the time to experience and work through her grief. She was able to share memories of Ralph that filled her with bittersweet feelings. She saw Ralph as a whole person with good and bad traits. She viewed their relationship in its entirety. While she still missed Ralph, she was beginning to look to the future and the rest of her life.

A year after terminating therapy, she reported that she had met a man who she fell head over heels for. It was a different relationship than the one she had had with Ralph, but it was still a very good one.

> Simona Sez . . .
>
> "When people in grief are not able to talk about their loved one, it is almost as painful as their loved one's death; the absence of conversation makes it feel like the person never lived!"

Family and friends are prone to avoid talking about the deceased because they are afraid that discussion of the departed will "upset" the bereaved. They are fooling themselves. They fail to realize that a person in grief is already upset and, due to their silence, suffering alone.

In addition, family members who remain silent about the deceased are trying to protect themselves. They too have suffered a loss and don't want to experience the grief that would surface for them. Friends who remain silent are protecting themselves from the pain they would feel about the losses in their life while talking about someone else's loss.

This is why it is so important to be surrounded by people who are sensitive to you and your loss when a loved one dies.

Case study:

Morris attended a bereavement support group after his wife of forty years died. He wanted to find a safe arena in which he could talk about his wife. He had tried to do so with his family, but they were too distraught with their own grief and could not tolerate their own feelings of loss or seeing Morris so upset.

In group, Morris talked about how much he missed Mildred and all that they had shared. After all, forty years was almost his entire adult life. He had cherished his life with her and at least wanted to revel in his memories. Morris was encouraged to share stories about Mildred and their life together. He shared with the group that it was very helpful to do so.

> Simona Sez . . .
>
> "With a major loss, there can be relentless aching and the feeling that your heart has been pulled out of your chest without the benefit of an anesthetic."

The pain of grief can feel unbearable; it is both unyielding and intense. In addition, it co-exists with other physical symptoms, as well as emotional, psychological, mental, intellectual, and behavioral symptoms. As a result, grievers sometimes self-medicate with alcohol or request prescriptions from their physicians for tranquilizers. Unfortunately, alcohol and drugs may anesthetize you and impede your ability to progress in your grief work, so both are best avoided.

Case study:

When Ian's wife died, family and friends rushed in to help. Ian talked about being unable to sleep and being anxious every time he thought about life without his wife. His sister gave him her prescription of Xanax to help calm his nerves. On top of that, a friend offered Ian his bottle of sleeping pills.

During his annual physical, six months after burying his wife, Ian's physician noticed that Ian was clinically depressed. After learning about Ian's use of Xanax and sleeping pills, he weaned Ian off of the medications and recommended psychotherapy.

The impact of his wife's death hit Ian full force now that he was no longer being anesthetized by drugs. A few weeks into his therapy, Ian made this statement: "You can run, but you cannot hide from grief – it will always be waiting for you when you are ready to deal with it."

Simona Sez . . .

"It is important for you to go through your deceased loved one's belongings."

There is really no "right time" to go through your loved one's belongings. You will probably want to sort through things gradually, as you will experience a lot of thoughts and feelings as you decide what to hold on to, what to give to others in the family, and what to give away. Having a supportive person with you will allow you to talk about what you are experiencing as you go through this process. This will assist you in your grief work.

Case study:

Jessica did not want to go through her husband's belongings after he died. Two years later, all of his things were left just the way they were prior to his death. Jessica did not want to accept that her husband had died and that he would never have the need to use his things again.

Jessica entered therapy because her sister recognized that Jessica was "stuck" in her grief and unable to function in a world without her husband.

> Simona Sez . . .
>
> "The expression of grief through crying can be a normal part of the grief process."

Not all grievers cry. Some grievers cry a lot in the early days after the death of their loved one. Other grievers try to be stoic and hold back their tears, while still others cry only in private.

Case study:

During a grief support group, Isaac, an elderly participant, shared that he had never cried during the Holocaust, not even when family and friends were killed in front of him. Now, with tears welling up in his eyes, he said that he could not stop crying since his wife's death six months ago. He reasoned that, because it was now safe to have feelings, it was as if a floodgate had opened and all the sadness and grief he experienced earlier in his life could no longer be contained.

Within the safety of the group, Isaac was able to rework his past losses in the context of the current loss of his wife.

> Simona Sez . . .
>
> "Use your journey to become the best possible you."

Working through your grief will strengthen your character, promote positive self-esteem, and provide you with a general feeling of emotional well-being.

Case study:

Anna was understandably devastated when her daughter died two years after being diagnosed with cancer. Anna had been her daughter's primary caregiver; now her time was filled with her grief. In the months following the funeral, Anna's feelings of devastation spiraled into unrelenting depression. Six months after her daughter's death, she entered therapy and began attending a grief support group.

While in therapy, Anna concluded that her current emotional state would not bring her daughter back. Nothing could change that reality. However, she knew she had to "do" something. While exploring what she could do, Anna decided to dedicate the rest of her life to raising both awareness of the illness that claimed her daughter's life and funds to find a cure for it.

This decision had an immediate impact on Anna – she felt a renewed sense of purpose. Both her depression and self-esteem lifted. Her new path allowed her to acknowledge her daughter's life as well as her death.

# INDEX

9/11, 16

AA meetings, 33

abandonment, 97

accept, 21, 44, 75, 97, 116, 123

acceptable, 6

acceptance, 52, 97, 108

aching, 120

acting out, 73

action, 55, 58

actions, 7

actively engage in new behavior, 22

admission, 67, 89

admonish, 27

admonished, 7

afraid, 7, 67, 118

aggressive, 11

alcohol, 6, 120

alcoholic, 21, 33, 36

alone, 7, 23, 29, 33, 52, 87, 97, 108, 118

anesthetize, 120

anesthetized, 121

anger, 35, 45, 73, 97

anger management, 5, 73

angry, 21, 25, 45, 46, 63, 73, 74, 83

anxiety, 5, 7, 13, 25, 29, 67

anxious, 5, 9, 13, 63, 83, 87, 97, 121

apologize, 73, 74

apology, 75

apprehensive, 29

appropriate, 11, 13

ashamed, 45

asserted, 77

assertive, 10, 11, 61

assumption, 63

assumptions, 62

attempted suicide, 7

attention, 14, 29, 60

attentive, 85

avoid, 12, 13, 113, 118

avoided, 77, 120

aware, 4, 43, 44, 68

awareness, 21

bad, 6, 14, 15, 16, 25, 28, 82, 117

badly, 81

balance, 36, 37, 112

barriers, 61

basic needs, 15

~ 133 ~

# INDEX

BE PRODUCTIVE, 12

behavior, 8, 10, 22, 23, 44, 45, 46, 52, 55, 60, 64, 65, 68, 69, 73, 77, 78, 90, 91, 97, 113

being, 4, 10, 11, 12, 25, 26, 28, 29, 33, 34, 35, 39, 42, 46, 47, 73, 76, 80, 81, 82, 89, 93, 94, 121, 126

being alone, 13, 29

being alone, 12

being fully engaged, 12

being happy, 12

being in the moment, 12

believing, 56

Bereavement support group, 111, 119

blame, 97

building blocks, 14

butterflies, 9

calmer, 9

caregiver's, 14

caregivers, 14

caring, 14

change, 22, 24, 32, 33, 34, 44, 47, 64, 65, 88

changes, 32, 33, 58, 107

changing, 39, 58, 88

chaotic, 21, 32

character, 126

"cheaters", 71

childhood, 28, 57, 78, 91

childhoods, 21, 97

childish, 74

choice, 31, 42, 89

choices, 30

clutter, 35, 52

co-dependent behavior, 90

comfort, 8, 13, 45

communication, 78

compassion, 8, 52, 81

compassionate, 21, 45

complaining, 53

completed suicide, 6

concern, 5

concerns, 23

concurrent responsibilities, 12

confided, 85, 125

confidence, 77

confront, 73

confronting, 65

confusion, 63

congruent, 18

connect feelings with thoughts, 19

# INDEX

consciously, 34, 42, 85

consumed, 36, 77

contemplated suicide, 21

contemplating, 4, 87

contradictory, 68

control, 14, 15, 16, 35, 42, 64

controlling, 35

controls, 14

conversation, 12, 27, 52, 54, 55, 59, 118

convinced, 69

cooperation, 52

couples, 62

crisis, 32, 33

critical, 25

criticized, 19, 25

crying, 19, 60, 77, 111, 124, 125

dead, viii, ix, 16, 21

dealing, ix, 78, 113, 127

death, 5, 16, 17, 41, 95, 109, 104, 105, 107, 111, 113, 116, 117, 118, 121, 123, 124, 127

decision, 15

decisions, 19, 44, 97

deescalated, 43

defend, 67

demands, 11, 52, 53

depressed, 14, 15, 21, 23, 121

depression, 21, 23, 25, 67, 107

details, 7

determine, 4, 31

determined, 5

developed, 21, 34, 41, 55, 81

die, 7

died, 17, 41, 105, 107, 109, 111, 113, 115, 119, 121, 123, 125, 127

diet, 37

differentness, 25

difficulties, 35, 41

disappointed, 46, 75

disappointment, 72, 73, 89

disapproval, 25

discovered, 39

disentangle, 67

dismissive, 65

disrespectfully, 23

distraction, 13

domineering, 35

Domino effect, 114

# INDEX

drinking, 21
drugs, 6, 23, 120, 121
dysfunction, 86
early experiences, 14
effective, ix
embrace the pain of grief, 112
emotional needs, 71
emotional pain, 85
emotional scars, 81
emotional strength, 76
emotionally intimate relationships, 21
emotionally vulnerable, 76
empathy, 85
emptiness, 57
emulating, 8
enabled, 19
encourage, 10
encouraged, 7, 29, 33
engage, vii, 10, 16, 21, 22, 39, 44, 46
enjoy, 13
enjoyed, 93
enjoying, 63
enjoyment, 16
Enron, 84
entangled, 66
entrusted, 9
envious, 93
escalate, 43, 45, 59
evaluate, 93
evaluating, 15, 92
examining, 59
exercise, 37, 112
expect, 22, 97
expectations, 35
expecting, 65
experience, 12, 19, 28, 29, 35, 44, 55, 57, 61, 67, 81, 91, 95, 107, 109, 110, 112, 117, 118, 122
experienced, 5, 28, 35, 41, 57, 89, 107, 125
experiences, 8, 14, 18, 19, 20, 21, 24, 28, 44, 89, 107, 108
experiencing, 4, 19, 62, 108, 111, 112, 122
exploded, 45
exploration, 55, 63, 97
explore, 45, 91, 97
explored, 23, 65, 89
exploring, 69
expressed, 25, 60, 61, 67, 73, 85, 91
expression, 10, 19, 35, 60, 76, 86, 97, 124

## INDEX

family, 5, 6, 16, 17, 25, 31, 35, 52, 53, 56, 67, 69, 87, 107, 109, 119, 121, 122, 125

fault, 7

fear, 7, 28, 29, 67, 97

feared, 5

feel, 4, 9, 14, 15, 22, 31, 38, 68, 71, 75, 76, 87, 90, 91, 97, 118, 120

feeling, 4, 13, 19, 21, 24, 25, 46, 55, 62, 77, 111, 120, 126

feelings, 5, 8, 12, 18, 19, 24, 25, 29, 35, 44, 45, 54, 55, 57, 59, 60, 61, 65, 67, 75, 76, 77, 81, 85, 89, 97, 110, 117, 122

felt, 5, 9, 15, 25, 27, 28, 29, 31, 45, 47, 54, 55, 57, 59, 67, 73, 79, 87, 111, 127

fidelity, 31

fight, 59, 106

fighting, 53

finances, 35

focus, 88

focusing, 89

foodaholic, 36

foundation, 14, 21

friend, 16, 61, 67, 107, 114, 115, 121

friends, 5, 6, 16, 17, 52, 56, 69, 91, 93, 109, 118, 121

frightened, 61

frustration, 24

fun, 52

go crazy, 31

go play in traffic, 21

goal, 81

goals, 46

good mental health, 18

good times, 16

gratification, 57

grief, 41, 104, 150, 107, 105, 107, 108, 109, 110, 111, 112, 117, 118, 119, 120, 121, 124, 125, 126, 127

Grief support group, 105, 107, 109, 127

grief work, 108, 120

grieve, 57, 89, 108, 109, 116

grow, 26, 34

grow up, 14

growing up, 15, 25, 60, 63, 67, 76, 77

~ 137 ~

## INDEX

guilt, 7

guilty, 79

happiness, 17

hats, 38, 39

health, 56, 57, 87

healthier, 31

healthy, 52, 53, 112

hear, 75, 76, 78

heard, 10, 27, 29, 43, 60, 64, 77, 78, 95

heartbroken, 17

herself, 9, 11, 13, 15, 19, 21, 35, 52, 53, 55, 57, 61, 65, 77, 85

hide, 68, 121

himself, 7, 25, 45, 47, 67, 73, 87

history, 63, 85, 91

home, 5, 7, 13, 23, 29, 31, 33, 37, 45, 51, 52, 53, 71, 75, 87, 91, 93, 109, 123

homes, 32, 52

honest, 46, 47, 81

honesty, 46

hooked, 67

hot potato, 82

humiliation, 67

hungry, 4

Hurricane Katrina, 16

hurt, 25, 59, 75, 85, 89

hurtful, 74

identify, 19, 57, 110

If I am not for myself, who will be for me?, 3

if only, 64, 65

ignore, 4

ignored, 60

imagined, 7

improve, 10

included, 95

incongruence, 47

incongruent, 19

incongruity, 69

individual, 22, 80, 109, 114

insecure, 67

insecurity, 97

insight, 85, 97

integrate, 18, 109

Integrity, 46

intelligence, 15

intense anxiety, 5

interaction, 59, 61, 63, 67, 79

interactions, 25, 84

interpretation, 25

interpreted, 55, 76, 77

interrupted, 59

intimate details, 6

# INDEX

invest, 84

invested, 92

investing, 84, 85

investment, 84, 85

issue, 25, 59

issues, 22, 24, 25, 37, 45, 55, 67, 72, 78, 87, 91, 92, 97, 123

Jessica McClure, 8

journaling, 110

journey, 126

just BE, 12

just being, 12

kill, 31

laughter, 19, 77, 78

learn, ix, 11, 17, 19, 24, 41, 57, 61

learned, 11, 13, 19, 21, 45, 77

learning, 121

"Let's Make a Deal", 30

lifelong, 97

listen, 16, 53, 119

listeners, 53

"little man", 67

loss, 17, 41, 89, 105, 107, 109, 104, 106, 108, 109, 110, 112, 114, 118, 120

losses, 89, 109, 104, 106, 107, 114

lovable, 14

love, ix, 23, 52, 56, 91, 95

loved, 35, 69, 95, 108, 114, 116, 118, 119, 122, 124

loving, 52

lovingly, 14

malicious, 74

marital, 33, 59

marriage, 33, 69, 71, 73, 115, 117

memories, 28, 104, 105, 117, 119

mental health, 18

mental illness, 6, 86, 112

messages, 6, 14, 76, 77

mirroring, 14

misunderstanding, 62

modulate, 11

mourn, 17

multiple roles, 12

mutual respect, 25, 52

needing, 95

needs, 4, 8, 15, 22, 39, 60, 91, 97, 115

nervous, 31, 40, 87

~ 139 ~

# INDEX

nervous breakdown, 31

no, 11

nonjudgmental environment, 28

nurture, 8, 52, 86

nurturing, 8

objectives, 46

Oklahoma City, 16

opportunities, 26

opportunity, 12, 25, 26, 28, 39, 51, 53, 74, 89, 104, 127

options, 31

ourselves, 4, 8, 12, 14, 44, 76, 94

overachiever, 35

overweight, 19

pain, ix, 28, 37, 112, 120

painful, 21, 118

painful experiences, 21

panic attacks, 57

parent's, 8, 104

parents, 7, 8, 13, 21, 25, 29, 35, 55, 87, 97

pathology, 21, 66, 67

patient, 54

patterns, 34

perceptions, 92

personality, 20, 108

perspective, 44, 76

physical soothing, 8

positive self-talk, 8

powerlessness, 64

practice, 10, 11, 12

practice makes everything easier, 10

"practice makes perfect", 10

practiced, 10

practicing, 10, 39

preparation, 5

prescriptions, 120

pressure, 10, 69

pride, 27, 46

privilege, vii

proactive, 5

problem, 45, 91

problems, 22, 23, 26, 36, 37, 45, 53, 65, 73, 85, 97

process, vii, ix, 32, 41, 44, 77, 110, 116, 122, 124

processes, 68

productive, 12

professional, 41

professions, 32, 95

progress, 120

# INDEX

protect, 118

psychopathology, 18

psychotherapy, 33, 57, 113, 121

psychotic, 31

quarreled, 7

Rabbi Hillel, 3

racially denigrating remarks, 27

racially disparaging remarks, 27

rage, 43, 45

rationalized, 37

realize, 37, 47, 59, 118

realized, 21, 31, 115

realizes, 22

reassuring, 9

recharge, 52

reciprocated vulnerability, 80

recognize, 19, 34, 45, 46

recognized, 11, 77

recognizing, 17

recovery, 65

refuel, 52

refueled, 52, 53

refueling, 5, 7, 51, 52

regret, 74

regulating, 14

rejection, 89

relationship, 20, 21, 22, 23, 39, 54, 55, 65, 81, 84, 85, 91, 97, 107, 109, 117

relationships, 45, 46, 47, 54, 80, 81, 85

relax, 53

relaxing, 53

remember, 29, 91

remembering, 56

repress, 19

resentful, 90

resentment, 91

resolve, 87, 91

respect, 25

respected, 95, 109

responses, 11

responsibilities, 12, 53, 93

responsibility, 4, 23

responsible, 7, 15, 16, 97

revealed, 55, 63, 65, 67, 77, 91

revealing, 77

ridiculed, 60

roles, 12, 114

run away, 31

# INDEX

sacrificed, 91
sad, 4, 85
sadness, 17, 29, 77, 105, 125
safe environment, 7
sarcastic, 59
sarcastically, 59
say no, 11
scared, 9
self-centered, 85
self-doubt, 67
self-esteem, 14, 21, 25, 87, 126
self-medicate, 120
self-talk, 8
sensitive, 110, 118
settle down, 9, 69, 73
sex, 6
shamed, 60
share, 6, 25, 62, 84, 89, 117, 119
shared, 5, 25, 33, 61, 63, 65, 67, 80, 119
sharing, 27, 85
shopaholic, 36
shut down, 25
silence, 12, 61, 118
silenced, 28
silent, 35, 61, 63, 118
sleep, 57, 61, 109, 121

sleeping pills, 121
soothe, 45
soothing, 8
strength, 52, 76, 112
strengths, 26, 27
stress, 23, 53, 61
stressed out, 23
stressful, 31
strong, 76, 77
stronger, 77
"stuffed", 19
struggle, 73
struggles, 97
stupid, 15, 19, 25, 77
suicide attempt, 6, 7
support, 39, 107, 108, 109, 110, 111, 119, 125, 127
supported, 17
support group, 125
supportive, 65, 122
taboo topics, 6
talk, 7, 28, 29, 39, 46, 53, 59, 77, 109, 118, 119, 122
talkable, 6, 55
talking, 63, 71, 110,
temper, 43, 73
tension, 53
terminated, 13

# INDEX

therapeutic, 54, 111

therapist, 54, 55, 77, 97

therapy, 7, 11, 13, 21, 22, 23, 25, 27, 28, 29, 45, 55, 57, 60, 61, 65, 71, 72, 73, 77, 81, 85, 87, 89, 97, 105, 107, 117, 121, 123, 127

thinking, 4, 62

thoughts, 5, 8, 12, 18, 19, 24, 29, 35, 44, 45, 60, 61, 110, 122

ticker tape, 62

tired, 4, 78

TO BE, 12

tool, 24

trauma, 28

traumatic experiences, 28

treatment, 19, 21, 63

triggered, 89

trust, 21, 52, 55, 76, 77, 80, 81, 85

trusting, 71

unacceptable, 27

uncluttered., 52

uncomfortable, 24

unconscious, 68

understand, 13, 21, 34, 35, 47, 55, 57, 65, 71, 75, 76, 93, 97, 111

understanding, 19, 41, 52, 72, 81, 85

unfaithfulness, 71

unhappiness, 22

unhappy, 74

unloved, 55

unrelated, 66

unresolved, 73, 112

unworthy, 15

upheaval, 73

upset, 8, 27, 45, 67, 71, 91, 93, 118

validate, 8

validating, 8

value, 9

values, 27, 46

verbalization, 5

verbalizing, 62

voice, 7, 27, 43, 60, 61

vulnerability, 77

vulnerable, 13, 54

weakness, 76

weaknesses, 26

weaned, 121

words, 42, 58, 60, 68, 69, 74

work, 19, 25, 31, 34, 37, 39, 45, 55, 73, 79, 81, 83, 87, 93, 95, 113, 116, 117, 123

~ 143 ~

## INDEX

work through, 55, 117, 123

workaholic, 36, 37, 113

worthiness, 15

worthless, 21

Xanax, 121

yourself, 46, 110